CANADA
FROM THE AIR

CLB 1596
© 1986 Illustrations and text: Colour Library Books Ltd.,
   Guildford, Surrey, England.
Text filmsetting by Acesetters Ltd., Richmond, Surrey, England.
Printed and bound in Spain.
All rights reserved.
ISBN 0 86283 437 6
Dep. Leg. B-5.249-86

CANADA
FROM THE AIR

CLIVE FRIEND

COOMBE BOOKS

Canada is one of the largest countries in the world, second only to the USSR, with an area of nearly 10 million square kilometres. It extends almost 5500 kilometres from the Yukon/Alaska frontier to Cape Spear in Newfoundland. When it was first suggested, the immediate thought was that it would prove a formidable task, attempting to photograph this vast area from a light aircraft with a cruising speed of little more than 100 knots. Coupled to this was the requirement that the photographs should also reflect the changing seasons, as a major aspect of life in most of Canada is the contrast between the hot and sometimes humid summer and the harsh beauty of winter.

The problem was tackled by dividing the assignment into three trips. In the winter of 1985 I set out to photograph the eastern cities from Thunder Bay to Quebec, and my colleague Neil Sutherland covered the northern cities of Yellowknife and Whitehorse together with Vancouver, the Coastal Mountains and the Rockies. This gave us a good cross-section of cities in winter plus a good representation of the winter sporting areas. I then returned in the following summer to cover many cities from Victoria to St. John's and as much as possible of the major variations of landscape within reasonable distance of the cities. It was, sadly, beyond our resources to venture on to the really far-flung regions like Baffin Island and Inuvik. However, we endeavoured to cover the areas where the vast majority of Canadians live and spend their recreation time.

The way we worked was to travel from one city to the next by scheduled airline and then to charter a light aircraft on the spot, either from the local flying club or from a local charter company. Our ideal aircraft for aerial photography is the Cessna 172, which combines reasonable comfort with adequate room to work (many of the photographs were taken on a 5x4 Linhof and the remainder on Hasselblad and Pentax 6x7 cameras, and these large instruments require a reasonable amount of elbow room to manipulate). The aeroplane has a maximum flying time of about five hours. This gives a range of about 600 miles or 960km, less the time

taken to circle the subject, which is likely to cut this by half. A typical day's flying would be about six hours flying time with a refuelling stop for aircraft and crew. One of the many considerations to be taken into account is the weakening effect of cold upon the bladder – there are no restrooms in a light aircraft! Indeed, on one memorable occasion we were cruising at 12,000 feet over the Rockies when the pilot suddenly asked if I had ever flown an aircraft. Fortunately I am capable of at least steering a straight and level course as he suddenly disappeared into the rear of the aircraft and had recourse to a convenient sick bag! I should add that we were a good two hours from the nearest airfield.

We begin our journey across Canada at Whitehorse, a city of 13,000 inhabitants and the capital of the Yukon. It is situated on the flat plane of the Yukon River below old river cliffs, above which runs the Alaska Highway. The modern city contrasts strongly with the stark beauty of the Yukon landscape, particularly on a fine day in the long, cold winter its citizens must endure. Permanently beached on the river-bank is the sternwheeler *SS Klondike*, which once plied the Yukon to Dawson. The journey took 40 hours downstream and 96 hours back against the current. South of the city is Miles Canyon, where the river flows between sheer, columnar, basalt walls.

We now move on to the south of British Columbia and the lovely city of Vancouver. It is superbly situated on a peninsula protruding west into the Strait of Georgia and bounded to the north by Burrard Inlet and to the south by the delta of the Fraser River. On the narrow northern shore of Burrard Inlet lies North Vancouver, above which tower the Coast Mountains. Further away to the south lie the Cascades of the United States of America. Unlike most regions of Canada the Vancouver area has little or no snow in the plain, although there is excellent skiing only a short drive from the city, on Grouse Mountain as well as further into the Coast Mountains. Vancouver has changed drastically during 1985 in preparation for Expo 86. Perhaps the most striking addition is Canada Place on the shore of Burrard Inlet between the seabus terminal and the ferry terminal. On the False Creek side lies B.C. Place, one of the world's finest covered stadia. The Expo site in fact occupies the whole north shore of Burrard Inlet from the main entrance and Expo Centre on Quebec Street to Granville Bridge. From the aeroplane we can also peer straight down onto Robson Square, in the heart of the City, or into the lovely sunken Gardens of Queen Elizabeth Park, or watch the ant-like crowds enjoying the fairground at the Pacific National Exhibition.

It is but a short hop by air south to Victoria, on the tip of Vancouver Island, the most southerly part of Western Canada. Victoria has the most temperate climate of the whole country and is, therefore, a major centre both for tourism and retirement. It is also the most English of Canadian cities. It originated as a Hudson's Bay Company trading post and was to become the Provincial Capital. The Pacific base of the Canadian Navy is situated a little to the north-east at Esquimault. The city has grown up around the harbour in James Bay, which today is busy with ferry boats from Vancouver, Seattle and the east coast of Vancouver Island.

From Victoria we now turn north up the craggy spine of Vancouver Island. To the east we can see Port Alberni at the head of Alberni Inlet, 12 miles from the Pacific Coast, and to the west lie row upon row of craggy ridges descending to the fog-shrouded Pacific Rim National Park. Our route now lies to the northwest across Strathcona Provincial Park and Buttle Lake and the teeming Islands in the Strait of Georgia to Bute Inlet, until at the head of the inlet we turn east into the valley of the Bishop River. On our left, away to the northwest, lies Mount Waddington which, at 4016m, is the highest point in the BC Coastal Mountains. We are now moving into the high glacier country of the Coastal Mountains and before us lies the Bishop Glacier, which starts its journey on the slopes of Lillooet Mountain 55) and descends into both the Bishop and Lillooet Valleys. It is a truly awe-inspiring sight as one circles gently over the high glaciers, peering down into the icy blueness of the myriad crevasses. One cannot help but think that this would be no place for an engine failure!

We now start back towards Vancouver along the wooded valleys northwest of Squamish, with the work of the foresters very much in evidence, past Garibaldi Lake and Mountain. In the distance lie the slopes which, in winter, become the skiers playground of Garibaldi Provincial Park and we carry on further north to Mount Whistler. Our return to Vancouver is now along Howe Sound, around Lighthouse Park and across Burrard Inlet.

The next leg of our journey takes us east of BC to Banff, in Alberta, the principal resort town of the Rocky Mountains. Here one can stay at the famous Banff Springs Hotel, perhaps the best known resort hotel in the country. To cover the Rockies I chartered a plane from the Calgary Flying Club, from where we flew along the route of the Bow Valley Parkway (Highway 1) to Banff. We were flying at about 5000 feet above the ground when it soon became apparent that we would have to be very much higher to obtain any kind of panorama across the peaks. I asked the pilot how high we could go, to which he replied '12000 feet in theory, but unless I can find a decent upward air current it will take a long time to get there because it is the operational ceiling of the aircraft'. He then headed straight for one of the sheer rock walls of the valley until it appeared to tower way above us. The aircraft was then put into an upward spiral until in a very short time we climbed above the main body of the mountains and the whole, wonderful panorama opened up before us. Such is one advantage of using a local pilot! We then flew on past Stanley Peak and Lake Louise before the gathering clouds forced us away from the mountains for a refuelling stop at Rocky Mountain House. After a brief rest (and not too much coffee!) we set off once more across the Albertan farmlands and past Gleniffer Lake to Drumheller. From here we followed the spectacular valley of the Red Deer River to the amazing scene of Dinosaur Provincial Park, which has yielded such spectacular fossil finds that it has been designated a World Heritage Site.

The shadows were now lengthening as we made a straight dash back to Calgary to catch the last rays of the setting sun on the downtown skyscrapers. Calgary is beautifully situated on the Bow River and in sight of the snow capped peaks of the Rockies. It was founded as a North West Mounted Police post over one hundred years ago, and with the coming of the railway soon became Canada's 'cow town'. This it has remained, but the cattle industry has been rapidly overtaken in importance since Calgary became the centre of the Canadian oil industry.

In contrast to the big business atmosphere of Calgary, Edmonton, the provincial capital, feels much more of a country town, with a quieter pace of life, although it, too, is much concerned with the agriculture and mineral resources of the province. The city sits on a plateau overlooking the North Saskatchewan River and the acres of parkland along the banks. It boasts the world's largest shopping and entertainment centre in the West Edmonton Mall, and a modern Convention Centre built into the river cliff.

From Alberta our journey east takes us across the vast prairies of Saskatchewan to the cities of Regina and Saskatoon. I was immediately struck by the strange pockmarks which dot the fields in this area. It turned out that these are alkali pans which form due to the close proximity of the water table to the surface. If they contain water it is of no use to man or beast due to the high salt content. This salt can sometimes be seen crystallized out around the edges or even over the whole surface. Their presence imposes a surreal pattern of harvesting upon the farmer, which can be most attractive. A completely unexpected aspect of flying over the Prairies was the consistently bumpy ride usually associated with hills. The pilot explained that this was due to the alternating cropped and ploughed fields. Whereas the dark, ploughed fields tend to absorb the heat of the sun, it is reflected by the light coloured fields of ripe crops, thereby producing an invisible pattern of ever-changing air density. The effect was rather like skimming across gently rippled water in a speedboat.

Far away to the north of the Prairies lies the capital of the North West Territories, Yellowknife. Set on the northern shore of the Great Slave Lake, the city is almost surrounded by water or, as in these pictures, by ice. In fact, during the winter, road access is directly across the frozen surface of Yellowknife Bay. The city takes its name not from the gold which is still mined today, but from the copper knives which were traded by the local Indians.

Returning to the Prairies we are now over the Province of Manitoba. No longer the tortuous harvesting patterns of Saskatchewan, but neat exercises in ruled lines characterise these fields. The area also appears much greener, but this can be attributed at least in part to the fact that, while Saskatchewan was enduring a severe drought at the time, Manitoba had been inundated by torrential rains. The capital of Manitoba is Winnipeg, situated at the confluence of the Assiniboine and Red Rivers. The city is something of a watershed in our journey, for not many miles to the east the Prairies come to an abrupt end, giving way to the lake and

forest country of the Canadian Shield. We have, in fact, crossed now into Ontario, for this is the Lake of the Woods, but it is a recreation area readily accessible to the people of Winnipeg. At the heart of this lakeland region is the beautiful resort of Minaki and a little further south the town of Kenora.

With an abrupt change of season we continue now to Thunder Bay on the northwest shore of Lake Superior. It is midwinter and the daytime high is -25° Celsius in still air. Smoke and steam is billowing from the chimneys of the Great Lakes Paper Mill at the foot of Mount McKay and the Bay itself is frozen solid across to the Sleeping Giant. Despite its position near the centre of the continent, Thunder Bay is one of the largest ports in Canada. Much of the grain from the Prairies arrives at the huge grain elevators on the lake shore before beginning the journey east along the St. Lawrence Seaway.

At the other end of Lake Superior lies Sault Ste. Marie on the narrow St. Mary's River, which also forms the frontier with the U.S.A. Here the cargo ships usually pass through one of the four giant American locks on their way to Lake Huron. The smaller passenger vessels are the main users of the single lock on the Canadian side. The 'Soo', with the giant Algoma Steelworks, is also an important industrial centre.

Further east, to the far side of Lake Huron, is Georgian Bay and the beautiful, island-studded Muskoka Lakes. From here we travel south over the pastoral farmland of southern Ontario, past Canada's Wonderland, until we meet Highway 401, the Toronto 'bypass' seen here at the intersection with the Don Valley Parkway. Toronto is the largest city in Canada, with a population approaching three million in the metropolitan area. Situated on the north shore of Lake Ontario, at roughly the half-way point on the St. Lawrence Seaway, Toronto is an important port as well as a major commercial centre. The city is dominated by the 1815ft CN Tower.

On the border with the province of Quebec is the Federal Capital – Ottawa. Superbly located on the bluff overlooking the Ottawa River are the Parliament Buildings. The city is bisected by the Rideau Canal, which in winter becomes one long ice rink, and a novel means of commuting for some of the people. A little to the northwest of Ottawa are the Laurentian Mountains, topped by Mont Tremblant which, at over 3000ft, is an excellent ski resort. Further east is Quebec's other top ski resort – Monte Sainte Anne, which is only a short distance from the provincial capital, Quebec City, the oldest city in Canada.

Quebec is built on a craggy cliff overlooking the St. Lawrence at the point where it starts to widen from river to estuary. On the cliff top is the Haute Ville (upper town), dominated by the Chateau Frontenac Hotel, and beneath is the Basse Ville (lower town) and the Levis ferry boat, which plies regularly back and forth across the St. Lawrence. The highest building in this view was used for the night shots because the exposure required was too long to shoot from an aircraft. The pictures of Quebec were in fact taken from a Jet Ranger helicopter, which made it easier to look down into the centre of the old town at the Snow Palace and sculptures of Carnaval. Just upstream of the city are the older, cantilever, Pont du Quebec and the modern, suspension, Pont Pierre Laporte spanning the ice-choked river.

Our last major hop takes us into the Maritime Provinces, to the city of Halifax, Nova Scotia. Halifax is built on a hill overlooking a deep inlet of the Atlantic Ocean, which forms one of the world's finest natural harbours. On top of the hill is the star-shaped Citadel and the Clock Tower. The Citadel is now a museum but, as Canada's Atlantic naval base, Halifax is still a military stronghold. Not far from Halifax there are many pretty towns and villages on the Atlantic coast, such as Prospect and Lunenburg. Turning inland we now cross to the north shore of New Brunswick and the lush Annapolis Valley, looking here along the snaking meanders to the Annapolis basin, where the river flows into the Bay of Fundy. Our route now crosses the Bay to the New Brunswick capital, Saint John, and continues along the coast to Port Elgin and Baie Verte, and across the Northumberland Strait to Prince Edward Island. We are met by a startling change of scenery, from the rugged Appalachians of Nova Scotia and New Brunswick to a gentle pastoral scene. This is because PEI was formed from the rich silt deposited by the glaciers which had scoured their way across the Appalachian Mountains. The Capital, Charlottetown, looks almost like a park from above, with its many trees and backdrop of cultivated fields. Just across the narrow waist of the Island is the P.E.I. National Park. Facing onto the Gulf of St. Lawrence are some of the finest sandy beaches in Eastern Canada.

The final province on our aerial journey is Newfoundland, the last rugged manifestation of the Appalachians. Our first view is of the spectacular Humber River Valley on the west of the island, and the forest and lake scenery which characterise the area. Further inland is Deer Lake. The Capital, St. John's, lies on the Avalon Peninsula sheltered from the Atlantic Ocean by the ancient rocks of Signal Hill. In the foreground is the narrow channel which leads into the fine harbour and, in the middle distance, the barely discernable passage to Quidi Vidi. Our last sight of Canada is Cape Spear, the most easterly point in the country, beyond which lies the open Atlantic Ocean and the lands which gave birth to the first settlers of this magnificent continent.

For the technically minded

All Neil Sutherland's pictures were taken on a Pentax 6x7 using the standard 100mm lens. I photographed every subject on a motorised Hasselblad Elm fitted with a meter prism and the standard 80mm lens for most shots, and a 150mm for the occasional closer view. Where time permitted and the shot justified it, I would ask the pilot to make one or more further orbits while I repeated the shot on the 5x4 Linhof, using either a 135mm or 210mm lens. The exposure was transferred from the Hasselblad meter. This proved much more reliable than attempting to use a hand held meter. Also the exposure varies considerably depending on the angle of view compared to the angle of the sun, so the reading must be taken from the same viewpoint as the photograph. In the high mountains, particularly in the snow, the exposures become incredibly short, perhaps as little as 1/500 sec at f16 on 100 ISO film. Also the pictures are much improved by the use of a polarising filter, which cuts the blue haze to a much greater degree than it does at ground level. Most of the pictures in this book were taken on Fuji 100 ISO reversal film. In general I uprate the film by 2/3 stop to 160 ISO for aerial work, otherwise the transparencies tend to look a bit flat.

Usually I prefer to fly at about 1500 feet above the ground. If the viewpoint is too high the pictures tend to look too map-like. A better perspective is obtained if the top of any very high points, such as the CN Tower in Toronto or the highest peaks in a mountain range, cut the horizon so as to appear with the sky as a background.

Yukon. Previous page, facing page and overleaf: the city of Whitehorse which, with a population of some 14,000, is the capital of the Yukon Territory. Permanently moored beside the Yukon River is the *SS Klondike*, which plied the river between Whitehorse and Dawson during the gold-rush days and now houses a museum. Above: the frozen Yukon River at nearby Miles Canyon.

Yukon. First appearing during the gold rushes of the 1890s, Whitehorse (these pages and overleaf) rapidly became an important transportation centre, a role which it still fulfils, as it was the head of navigation on the Yukon and also a railhead.

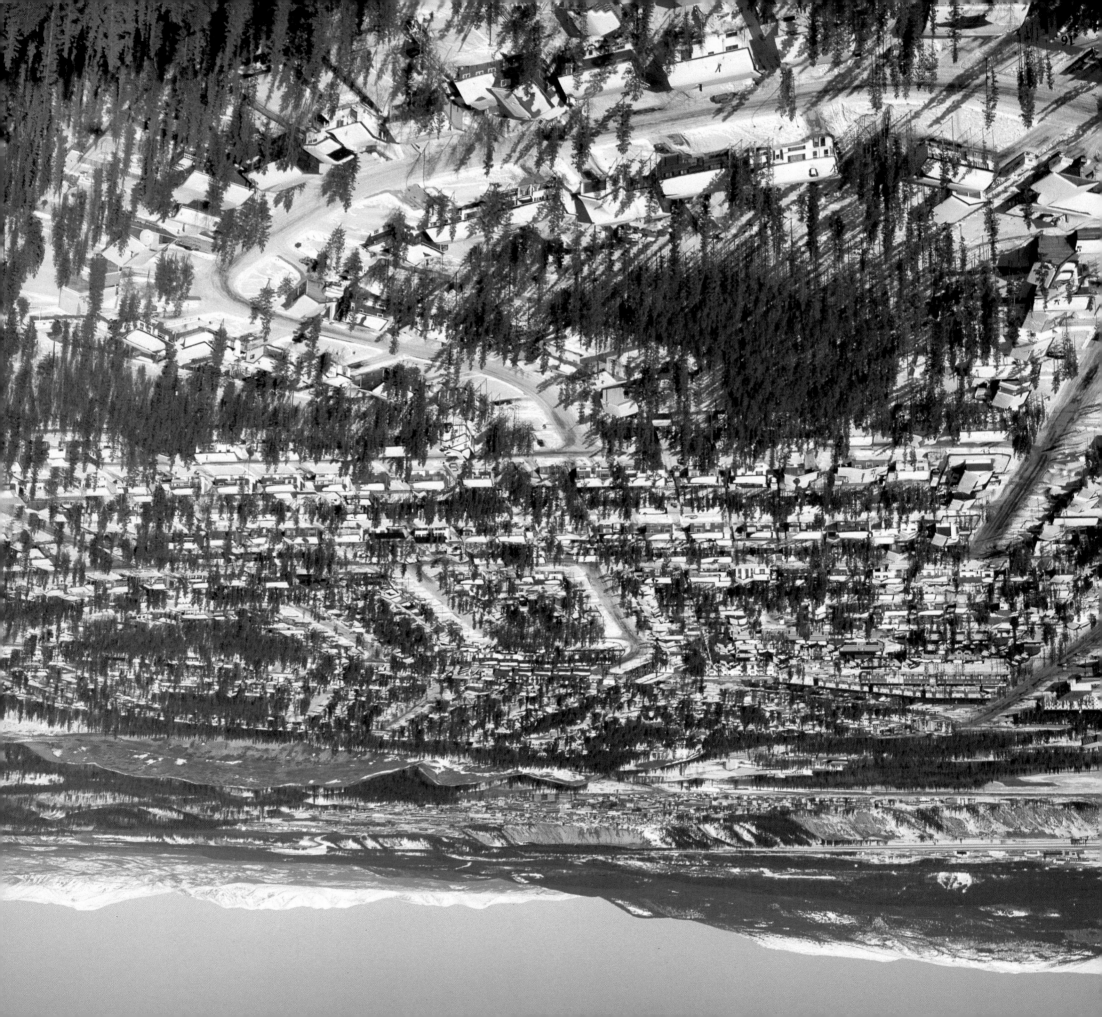

British Columbia. Vancouver is the largest city on the west coast and one of the most important ports in the nation.
Above: Vancouver and Burrard Inlet from above West Vancouver. Facing page: the city centre and Canada Place. Overleaf:
(left) Robson Square and (right) the city centre from the south.

Vancouver, British Columbia. Facing page: the colourful scene and exciting rides of the Pacific National Exhibition and (above) the remarkable triodetic dome of the Bloedel Conservatory in Queen Elizabeth Park.

Vancouver, British Columbia. Above: the city centre and Canada Place. Facing page: Granville Island Marina lies between Granville Bridge and Burrard Bridge as they cross False Creek. Overleaf: (left) Lighthouse Park and Point Atkinson and (right) the city centre and Burrard Inlet from the west.

British Columbia. Previous pages: the Simon Fraser University, beautifully positioned on Burnaby Mountain, is famous for
its architecture as well as its academic standing. These pages and overleaf: the harbour of Victoria, on Vancouver
Island, is overlooked by the domed Parliament Building of 1898 and the gabled Empress Hotel.

British Columbia. Facing page: the Coast Mountains west of Squamish. Above: the Coast Mountains south of the Upper Lillooet Valley. Overleaf: (left) Port Alberni, where the province's first paper mill was opened in 1894, and (right) mountains near the west coast of Vancouver Island.

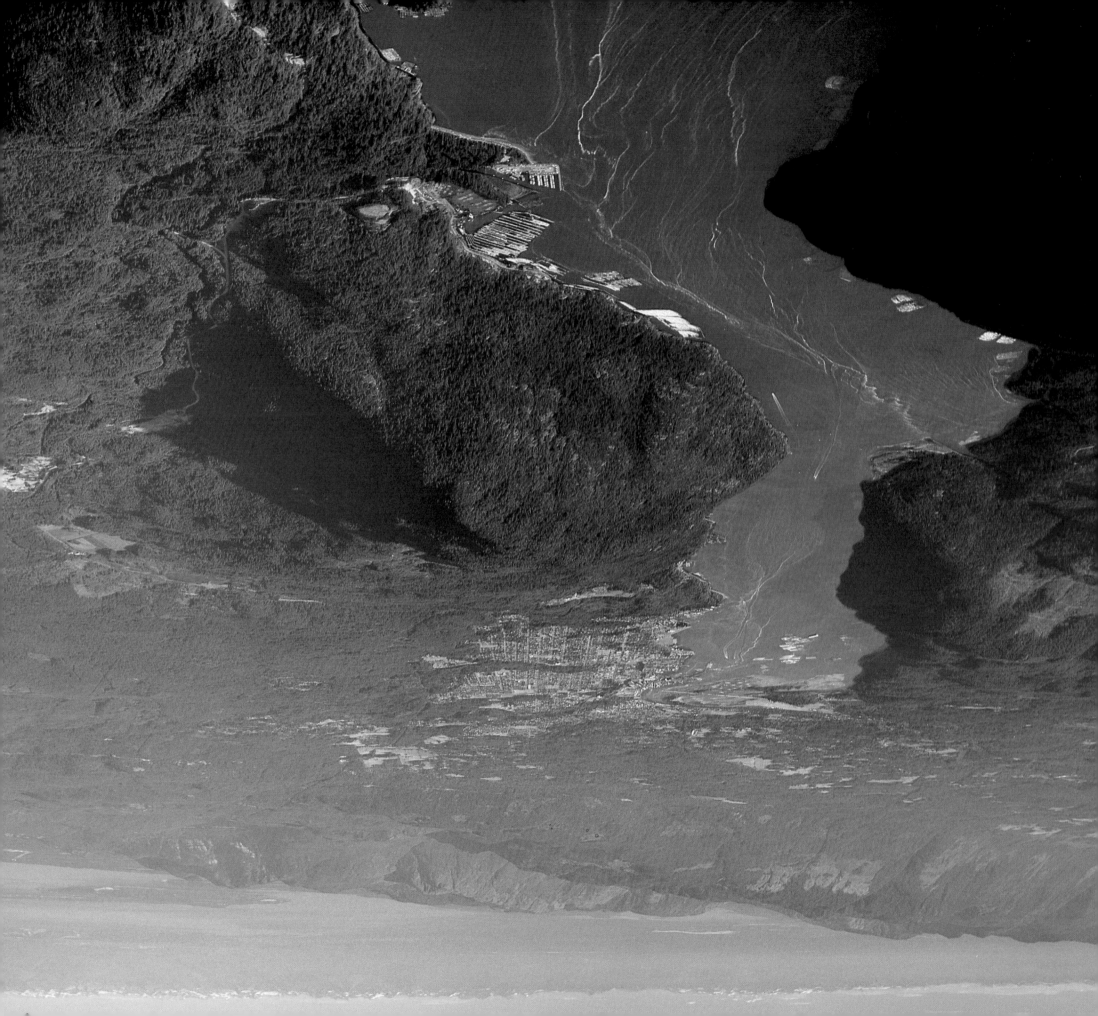

British Columbia. The mountains of the province are among the most beautiful in Canada. Above: peaks near the Elaho Valley. Facing page: timber stands north of Squamish. Overleaf: the Rockies between Squamish and Mount Whistler.

British Columbia. Facing page: Garibaldi Lake in the mountain scenery of Garibaldi Provincial Park. Above: the Squamish River Valley north of Brackendale. Overleaf: nearby mountain scenery.

British Columbia. These pages: the sharp peak of Mount Assiniboine, set in its own Provincial Park, punctures the skyline. Overleaf: (left) a ski resort and (right) mountain scenery, both near Mount Whistler.

British Columbia. Above: the Mount Whistler Ski Resort, one of the most popular in the province. Facing page and overleaf: ski centres between Squamish and Pemberton.

British Columbia. Above and overleaf left: glaciers near Pemberton. Facing page: the Bishop Glacier near the Lillooet Valley. Overleaf right: the head of the Lillooet Glacier.

British Columbia. Above and overleaf right: the Lillooet Glacier. Facing page: the Bishop River. Overleaf left: the view south from the Upper Lillooet Valley.

British Columbia. Facing page: Upper Campbell Lake in the foreground, with Buttle Lake beyond, on Vancouver Island.
Above and overleaf: Bute Inlet.

British Columbia. Above: Mount Waddington, the highest peak in the Coast Mountains, from the southeast. Facing page: distant Mount Waddington from above Bute Inlet.

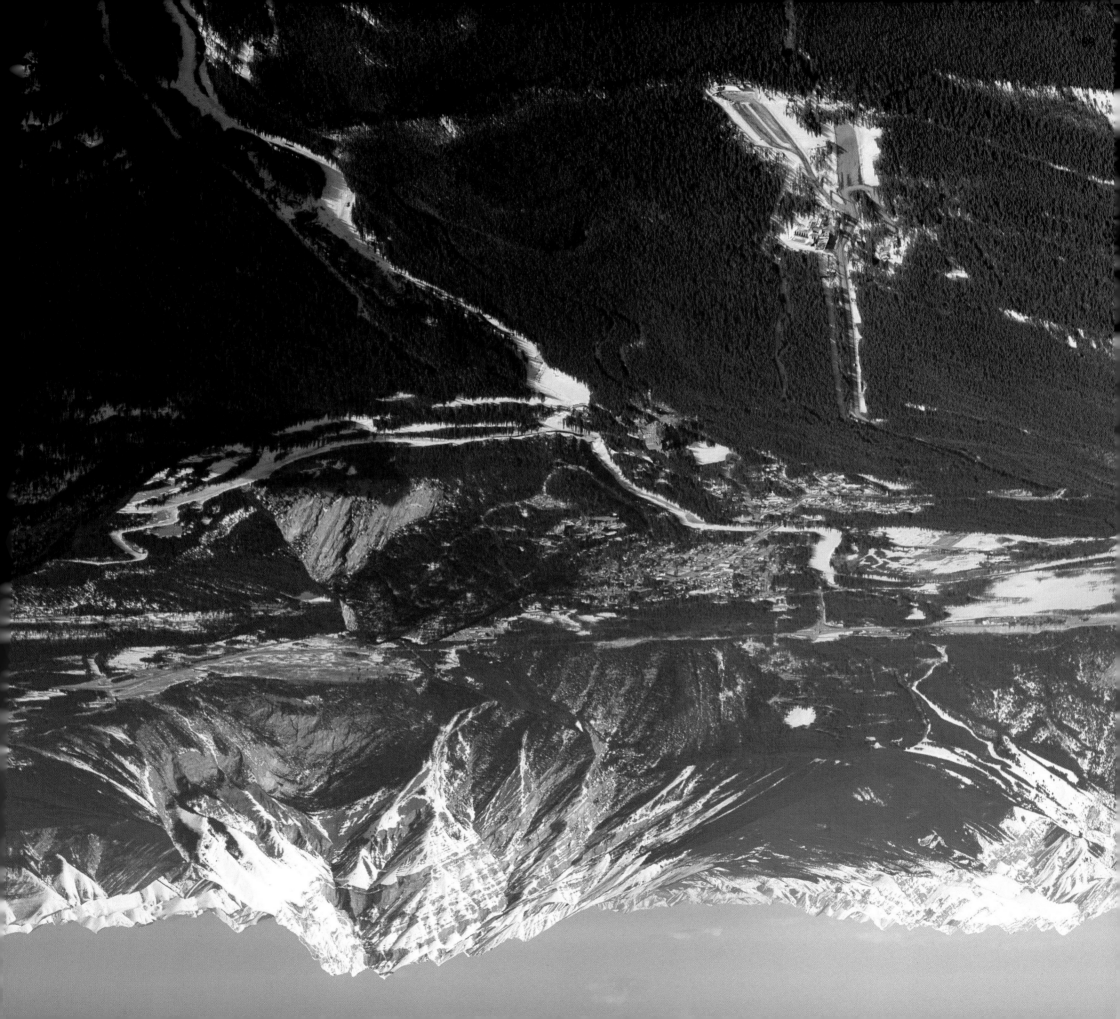

Alberta. Previous pages: (left) Banff townsite, with the clearing of Upper Hot Springs in the foreground and (right) the circular platform of the terminal of the Mount Sulphur gondola with Banff townsite beyond. Above: Canmore, a fishing and golfing resort west of Calgary. Facing page: the nearby Spray Lakes Reservoir. Overleaf: (left) Cascade Mountain and Tunnel Mountain tower above Banff townsite and (right) Highway 93 snakes along a frozen mountain valley near Banff.

Alberta. These pages: the jagged peaks and forested slopes of the Colorado Rockies. Overleaf: (left) Banff National Park and (right) an interchange on the Trans-Canada Highway near Canmore.

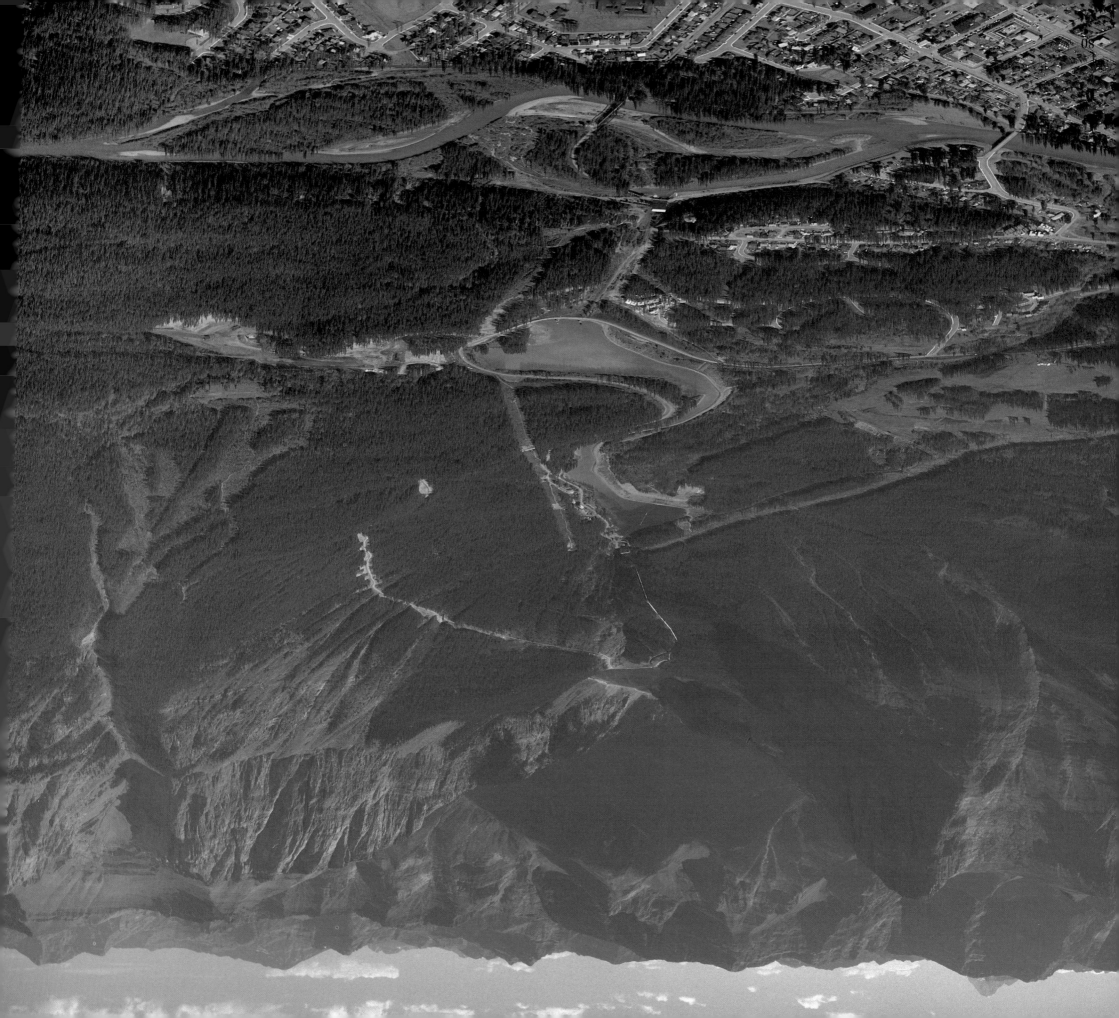

Alberta. Previous pages: (left) Stanley Peak and (right) Lake Louise. Facing page: Canmore, which lies nestled between peaks on the banks of the Bow River. Above: the dramatic mountain scenery around Stanley Peak. Overleaf: Calgary, showing (left) Calgary Heritage Park and the Glenmore Reservoir, and (right) the racetrack, grandstand and other buildings of Stampede Park, where the famous Calgary Stampede bursts its Western excitement upon the city every July.

81

Alberta. Calgary (these pages and overleaf) was founded as a fort of the North West Mounted Police in 1875 and has grown with startling speed in the intervening years. It is now a bustling city of some 700,000 inhabitants, chiefly concerned with the oil business and with serving the surrounding agricultural area.

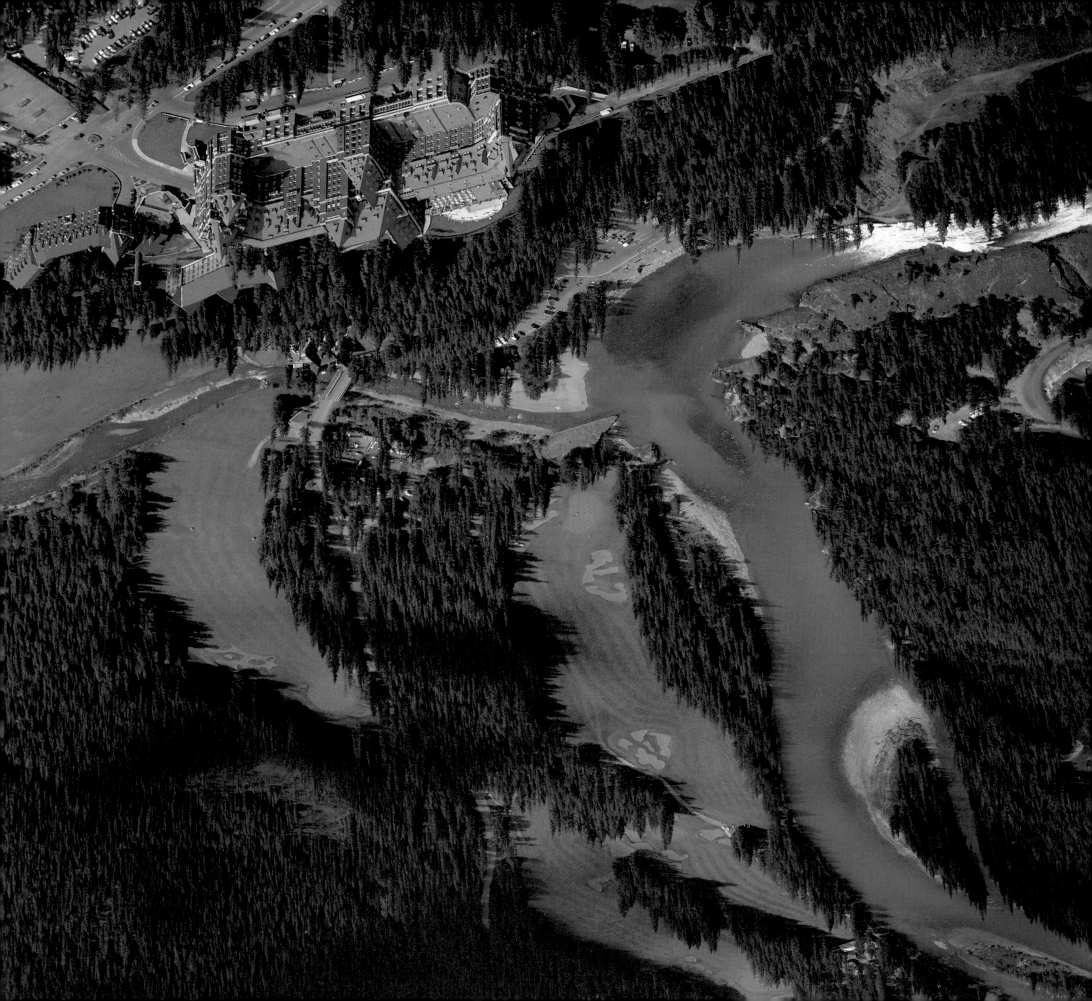

Alberta. Previous pages: (left) the palatial Banff Springs Hotel on the banks of the Bow River and (right) Dinosaur Provincial Park, north of Brooks, where many fossils have been found. Facing page: rich farmland near the Medicine River, east of Rocky Mountain House, and (above) near Drumheller. Overleaf: fertile farmland and deeply eroded river gullies near Drumheller.

Alberta. These pages: the running waters of the Red Deer River, a tributary of the South Saskatchewan River, which rises near Mount St. Bride, have cut a deep channel through the fertile farmland around Drumheller.

Alberta. Edmonton (these pages and overleaf) began as an outpost of the Hudson's Bay Company in 1795, but suffered fluctuations in fortune, including being abandoned twice, until a new fort was built on the site of the present-day Legislative Building (overleaf right). Since the arrival of the railway in 1891, the city has continued to expand, its latest spectacular acquisition being the West Edmonton Mall (overleaf left).

Alberta. The position of Edmonton (previous pages and these pages) near the limit of the mixed farming belt makes it the centre not only for its surrounding agricultural land and oilfields, but also for the entire northwest of the country. One of the city's chief sights is the Legislative Building (previous pages right, and above) which was completed in 1912 using Canadian, American and Italian marble.

Saskatchewan. Previous pages: (left) sandbanks divide the flow of the Saskatchewan River near Saskatoon, and (right) grain elevators at Broderick. Above: the blue waters of the 50-mile-long Last Mountain Lake, which stretches across the prairies north of Regina. Facing page: the flat lands near Holdfast.

...askatchewan. The two largest cities in the province, Saskatoon and Regina, lie in different agricultural belts, a fact ...hown in their economic roles, for while the former is engaged in general food processing, the latter houses one of the ...lobe's largest grain-handling organisations. Facing page and overleaf right: Saskatoon. Above and overleaf left: ...egina, with the domed Legislative Building, built in 1912 of Manitoban limestone.

Saskatchewan. It was the rich farming land of the prairies that attracted the hundreds of thousands of immigrants to the prairies between 1885 and the outbreak of World War I. The farming of the land is still of vital importance to the economy of the region and to the food supplies of the world. Facing page and overleaf left: near Fort Qu'Appelle. Above: a combine harvester near Broderick. Overleaf right: fields near Holdfast.

Northwest Territories. With a population of around 10,000, Yellowknife (previous pages right and overleaf) is the largest settlement in the territories as well as their capital. When winter grips the region, the Great Slave Lake freezes to such an extent that a road capable of carrying motor traffic (previous pages left and facing page) is built across the lake to Detah (above), a Dogrib Indian settlement.

Northwest Territories. Mining (above) is the main business of Yellowknife (these pages and overleaf) and was responsible for the two booms in the town's development. The first came in 1934 and resulted in the 'old town' on the narrow neck of land (background, overleaf left), while the second boom, that of the 1950s, created the new town with its more modern buildings (overleaf).

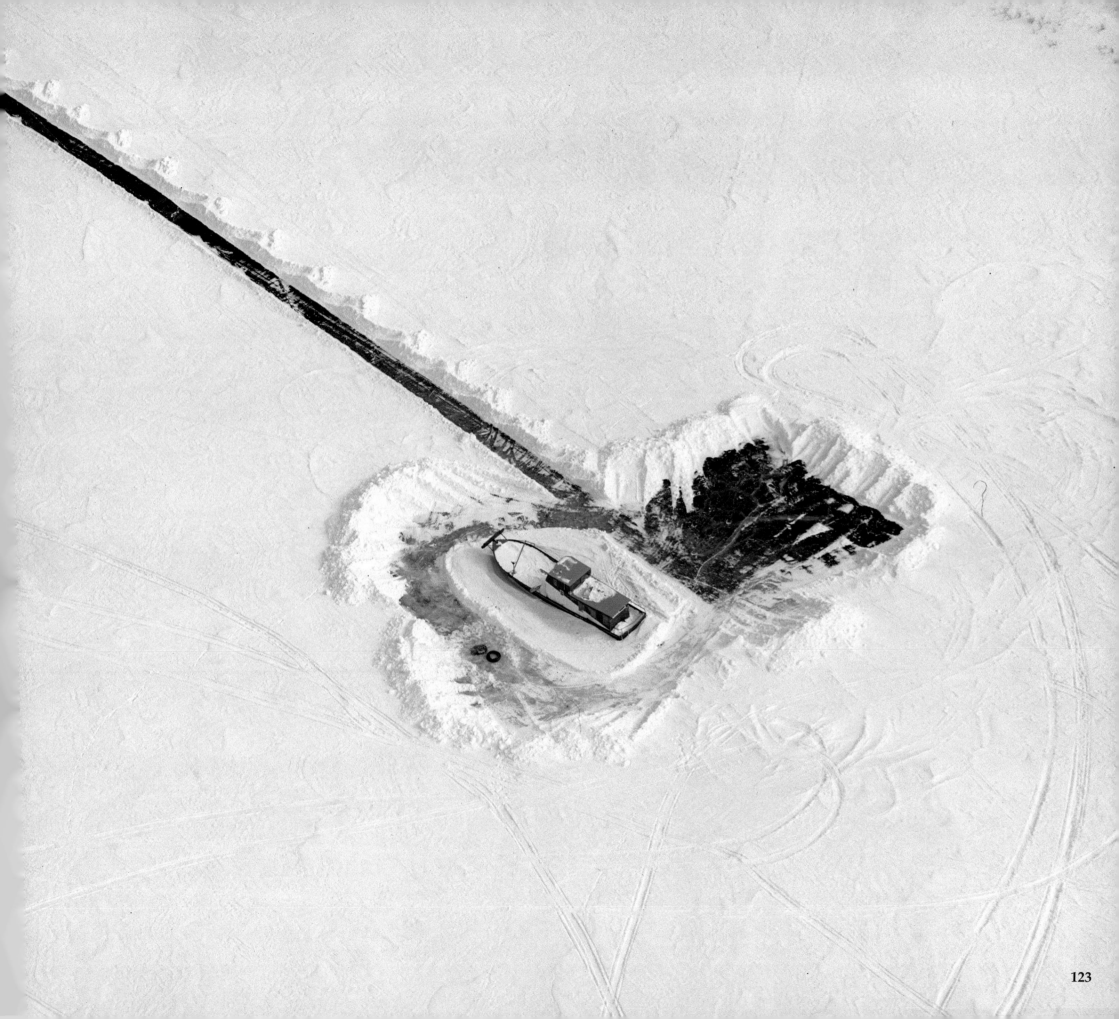

123

CLB 1596
© 1986 Illustrations and text: Colour Library Books Ltd.,
    Guildford, Surrey, England.
Text filmsetting by Acesetters Ltd., Richmond, Surrey, England.
Printed and bound in Spain.
All rights reserved.
ISBN 0 86283 437 6
Dep. Leg. B-5.249-86

seabus terminal and the ferry terminal. On the False Creek side lies B.C. Place, one of the world's finest covered stadia. The Expo site in fact occupies the whole north shore of Burrard Inlet from the main entrance and Expo Centre on Quebec Street to Granville Bridge. From the aeroplane we can also peer straight down onto Robson Square, in the heart of the City, or into the lovely sunken Gardens of Queen Elizabeth Park, or watch the ant-like crowds enjoying the fairground at the Pacific National Exhibition.

It is but a short hop by air south to Victoria, on the tip of Vancouver Island, the most southerly part of Western Canada. Victoria has the most temperate climate of the whole country and is, therefore, a major centre both for tourism and retirement. It is also the most English of Canadian cities. It originated as a Hudson's Bay Company trading post and was to become the Provincial Capital. The Pacific base of the Canadian Navy is situated a little to the north-east at Esquimault. The city has grown up around the harbour in James Bay, which today is busy with ferry boats from Vancouver, Seattle and the east coast of Vancouver Island.

From Victoria we now turn north up the craggy spine of Vancouver Island. To the east we can see Port Alberni at the head of Alberni Inlet, 12 miles from the Pacific Coast, and to the west lie row upon row of craggy ridges descending to the fog-shrouded Pacific Rim National Park. Our route now lies to the northwest across Strathcona Provincial Park and Buttle Lake and the teeming Islands in the Strait of Georgia to Bute Inlet, until at the head of the inlet we turn east into the valley of the Bishop River. On our left, away to the northwest, lies Mount Waddington which, at 4016m, is the highest point in the BC Coastal Mountains. We are now moving into the high glacier country of the Coastal Mountains and before us lies the Bishop Glacier, which starts its journey on the slopes of Lillooet Mountain 55) and descends into both the Bishop and Lillooet Valleys. It is a truly awe-inspiring sight as one circles gently over the high glaciers, peering down into the icy blueness of the myriad crevasses. One cannot help but think that this would be no place for an engine failure!

We now start back towards Vancouver along the wooded valleys northwest of Squamish, with the work of the foresters very much in evidence, past Garibaldi Lake and Mountain. In the distance lie the slopes which, in winter, become the skiers playground of Garibaldi Provincial Park and we carry on further north to Mount Whistler. Our return to Vancouver is now along Howe Sound, around Lighthouse Park and across Burrard Inlet.

The next leg of our journey takes us east of BC to Banff, in Alberta, the principal resort town of the Rocky Mountains. Here one can stay at the famous Banff Springs Hotel, perhaps the best known resort hotel in the country. To cover the Rockies I chartered a plane from the Calgary Flying Club, from where we flew along the route of the Bow Valley Parkway (Highway 1) to Banff. We were flying at about 5000 feet above the ground when it soon became apparent that we would have to be very much higher to obtain any kind of panorama across the peaks. I asked the pilot how high we could go, to which he replied '12000 feet in theory, but unless I can find a decent upward air current it will take a long time to get there because it is the operational ceiling of the aircraft'. He then headed straight for one of the sheer rock walls of the valley until it appeared to tower way above us. The aircraft was then put into an upward spiral until in a very short time we climbed above the main body of the mountains and the whole, wonderful panorama opened up before us. Such is one advantage of using a local pilot! We then flew on past Stanley Peak and Lake Louise before the gathering clouds forced us away from the mountains for a refuelling stop at Rocky Mountain House. After a brief rest (and not too much coffee!) we set off once more across the Albertan farmlands and past Gleniffer Lake to Drumheller. From here we followed the spectacular valley of the Red Deer River to the amazing scene of Dinosaur Provincial Park, which has yielded such spectacular fossil finds that it has been designated a World Heritage Site.

The shadows were now lengthening as we made a straight dash back to Calgary to catch the last rays of the setting sun on the downtown skyscrapers. Calgary is beautifully situated on the Bow River and in sight of the snow capped peaks of the Rockies. It was founded as a North West Mounted Police post over one hundred years ago, and with the coming of the railway soon became Canada's 'cow town'. This it has remained, but the cattle industry has been rapidly overtaken in importance since Calgary became the centre of the Canadian oil industry.

In contrast to the big business atmosphere of Calgary, Edmonton, the provincial capital, feels much more of a country town, with a quieter pace of life, although it, too, is other top ski resort – Monte Sainte Anne, which is only a short distance from the provincial capital, Quebec City, the oldest city in Canada.

Quebec is built on a craggy cliff overlooking the St. Lawrence at the point where it starts to widen from river to estuary. On the cliff top is the Haute Ville (upper town), dominated by the Chateau Frontenac Hotel, and beneath is the Basse Ville (lower town) and the Levis ferry boat, which plies regularly back and forth across the St. Lawrence. The highest building in this view was used for the night shots because the exposure required was too long to shoot from an aircraft. The pictures of Quebec were in fact taken from a Jet Ranger helicopter, which made it easier to look down into the centre of the old town at the Snow Palace and sculptures of Carnaval. Just upstream of the city are the older, cantilever, Pont du Quebec and the modern, suspension, Pont Pierre Laporte spanning the ice-choked river.

Our last major hop takes us into the Maritime Provinces, to the city of Halifax, Nova Scotia. Halifax is built on a hill overlooking a deep inlet of the Atlantic Ocean, which forms one of the world's finest natural harbours. On top of the hill is the star-shaped Citadel and the Clock Tower. The Citadel is now a museum but, as Canada's Atlantic naval base, Halifax is still a military stronghold. Not far from Halifax there are many pretty towns and villages on the Atlantic coast, such as Prospect and Lunenburg. Turning inland we now cross to the north shore of New Brunswick and the lush Annapolis Valley, looking here along the snaking meanders to the Annapolis basin, where the river flows into the Bay of Fundy. Our route now crosses the Bay to the New Brunswick capital, Saint John, and continues along the coast to Port Elgin and Baie Verte, and across the Northumberland Strait to Prince Edward Island. We are met by a startling change of scenery, from the rugged Appalachians of Nova Scotia and New Brunswick to a gentle pastoral scene. This is because PEI was formed from the rich silt deposited by the glaciers which had scoured their way across the Appalachian Mountains. The Capital, Charlottetown, looks almost like a park from above, with its many trees and backdrop of cultivated fields. Just across the narrow waist of the Island is the P.E.I. National Park. Facing onto the Gulf of St. Lawrence are some of the finest sandy beaches in Eastern Canada.

The final province on our aerial journey is Newfoundland, the last rugged manifestation of the Appalachians. Our first view is of the spectacular Humber River Valley on the west of the island, and the forest and lake scenery which characterise the area. Further inland is Deer Lake. The Capital, St. John's, lies on the Avalon Peninsula sheltered from the Atlantic Ocean by the ancient rocks of Signal Hill. In the foreground is the narrow channel which leads into the fine harbour and, in the middle distance, the barely discernable passage to Quidi Vidi. Our last sight of Canada is Cape Spear, the most easterly point in the country, beyond which lies the open Atlantic Ocean and the lands which gave birth to the first settlers of this magnificent continent.

For the technically minded

All Neil Sutherland's pictures were taken on a Pentax 6x7 using the standard 100mm lens. I photographed every subject on a motorised Hasselblad Elm fitted with a meter prism and the standard 80mm lens for most shots, and a 150mm for the occasional closer view. Where time permitted and the shot justified it, I would ask the pilot to make one or more further orbits while I repeated the shot on the 5x4 Linhof, using either a 135mm or 210mm lens. The exposure was transferred from the Hasselblad meter. This proved much more reliable than attempting to use a hand held meter. Also the exposure varies considerably depending on the angle of view compared to the angle of the sun, so the reading must be taken from the same viewpoint as the photograph. In the high mountains, particularly in the snow, the exposures become incredibly short, perhaps as little as 1/500 sec at f16 on 100 ISO film. Also the pictures are much improved by the use of a polarising filter, which cuts the blue haze to a much greater degree than it does at ground level. Most of the pictures in this book were taken on Fuji 100 ISO reversal film. In general I uprate the film by 2/3 stop to 160 ISO for aerial work, otherwise the transparencies tend to look a bit flat.

Usually I prefer to fly at about 1500 feet above the ground. If the viewpoint is too high the pictures tend to look too map-like. A better perspective is obtained if the top of any very high points, such as the CN Tower in Toronto or the highest peaks in a mountain range, cut the horizon so as to appear with the sky as a background.

Yukon. Previous page, facing page and overleaf: the city of Whitehorse which, with a population of some 14,000, is the capital of the Yukon Territory. Permanently moored beside the Yukon River is the *SS Klondike*, which plied the river between Whitehorse and Dawson during the gold-rush days and now houses a museum. Above: the frozen Yukon River at nearby Miles Canyon.

Yukon. First appearing during the gold rushes of the 1890s, Whitehorse (these pages and overleaf) rapidly became an important transportation centre, a role which it still fulfils, as it was the head of navigation on the Yukon and also a railhead.

British Columbia. Vancouver is the largest city on the west coast and one of the most important ports in the nation.
Above: Vancouver and Burrard Inlet from above West Vancouver. Facing page: the city centre and Canada Place. Overleaf:
(left) Robson Square and (right) the city centre from the south.

Vancouver, British Columbia. Above: the city centre and Canada Place. Facing page: Granville Island Marina lies between Granville Bridge and Burrard Bridge as they cross False Creek. Overleaf: (left) Lighthouse Park and Point Atkinson and (right) the city centre and Burrard Inlet from the west.

British Columbia. Previous pages: the Simon Fraser University, beautifully positioned on Burnaby Mountain, is famous for
its architecture as well as its academic standing. These pages and overleaf: the harbour of Victoria, on Vancouver
Island, is overlooked by the domed Parliament Building of 1898 and the gabled Empress Hotel.

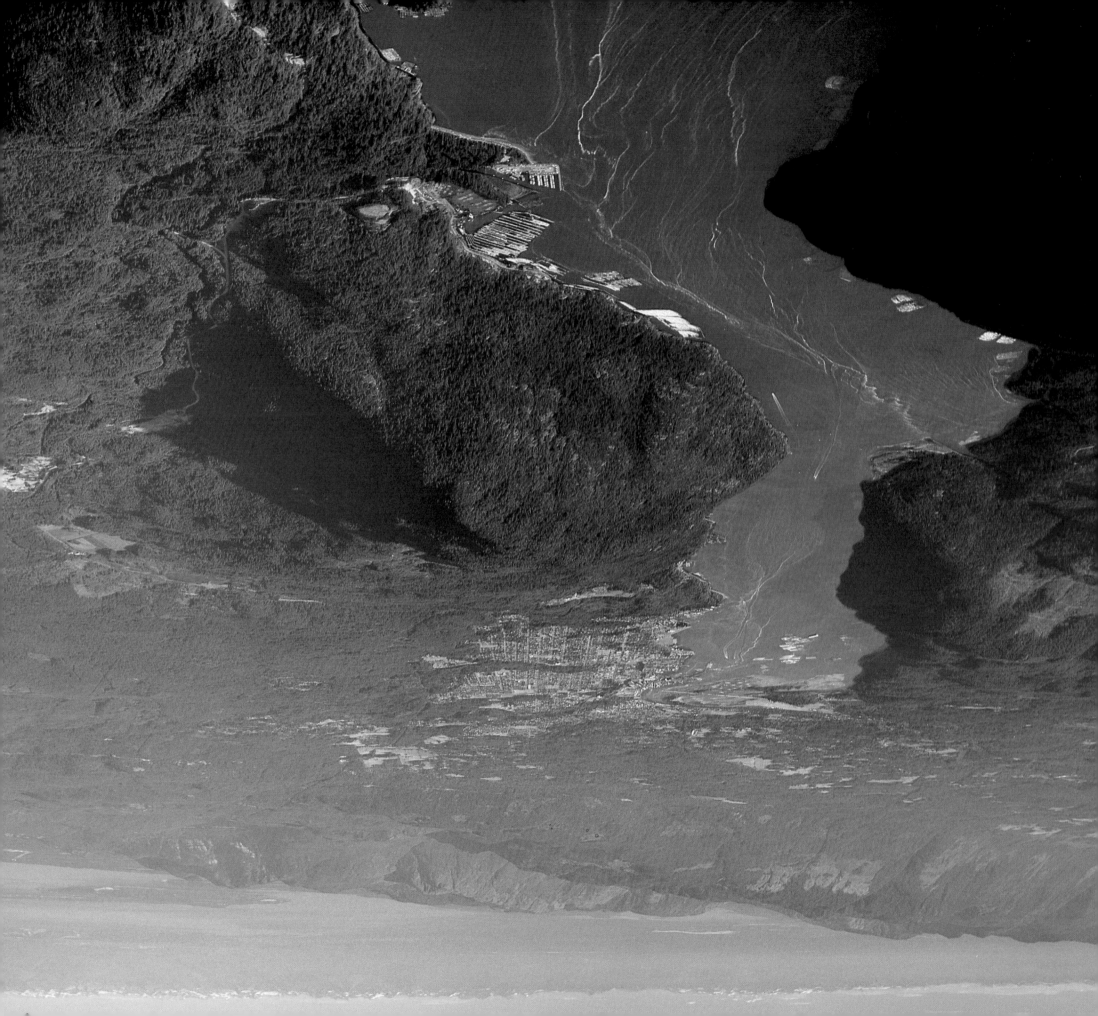

British Columbia. The mountains of the province are among the most beautiful in Canada. Above: peaks near the Elaho Valley. Facing page: timber stands north of Squamish. Overleaf: the Rockies between Squamish and Mount Whistler.

British Columbia. These pages: the sharp peak of Mount Assiniboine, set in its own Provincial Park, punctures the skyline. Overleaf: (left) a ski resort and (right) mountain scenery, both near Mount Whistler.

British Columbia. Above and overleaf left: glaciers near Pemberton. Facing page: the Bishop Glacier near the Lillooet Valley. Overleaf right: the head of the Lillooet Glacier.

British Columbia. Above and overleaf right: the Lillooet Glacier. Facing page: the Bishop River. Overleaf left: the view south from the Upper Lillooet Valley.

British Columbia. Above: Mount Waddington, the highest peak in the Coast Mountains, from the southeast. Facing page: distant Mount Waddington from above Bute Inlet.

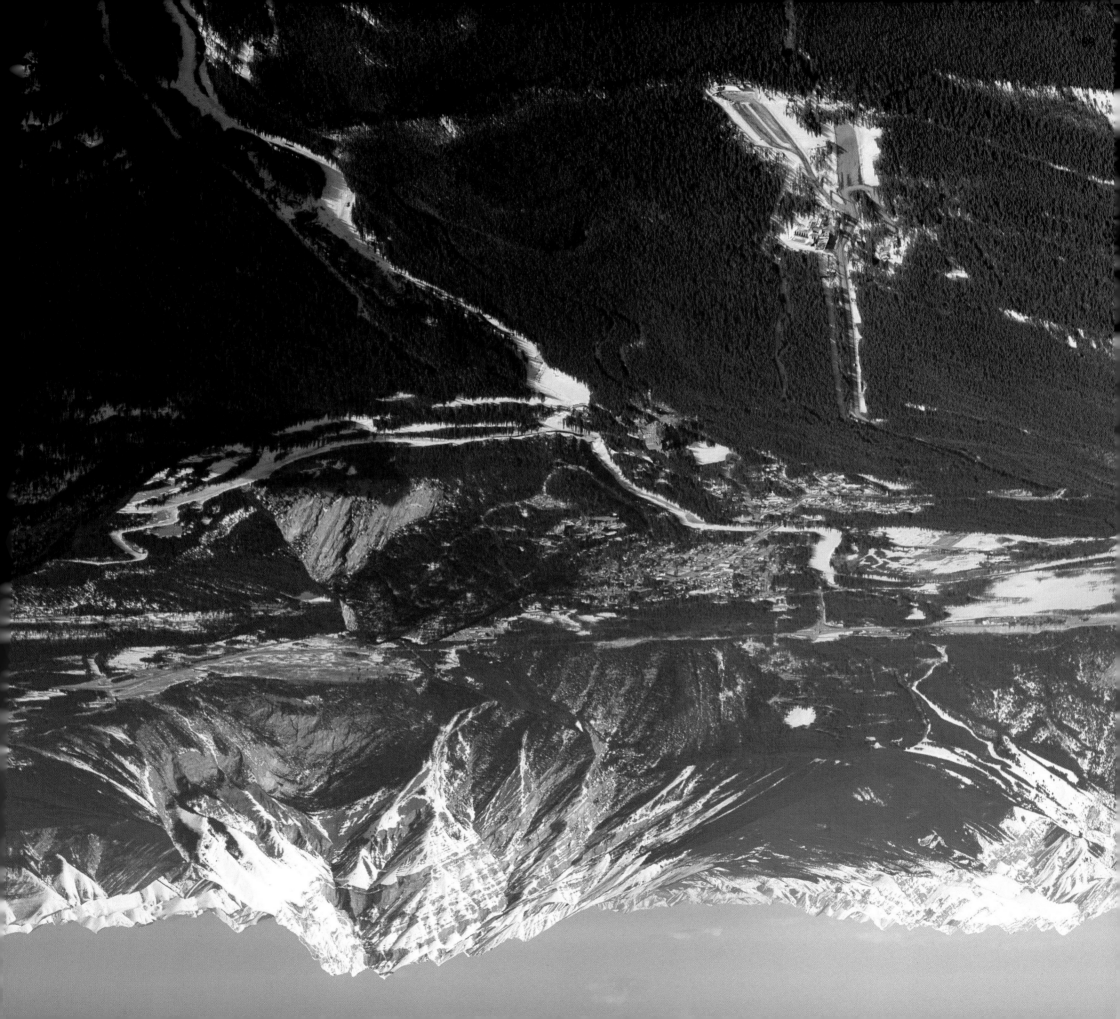

Alberta. Previous pages: (left) Banff townsite, with the clearing of Upper Hot Springs in the foreground and (right) the circular platform of the terminal of the Mount Sulphur gondola with Banff townsite beyond. Above: Canmore, a fishing and golfing resort west of Calgary. Facing page: the nearby Spray Lakes Reservoir. Overleaf: (left) Cascade Mountain and Tunnel Mountain tower above Banff townsite and (right) Highway 93 snakes along a frozen mountain valley near Banff.

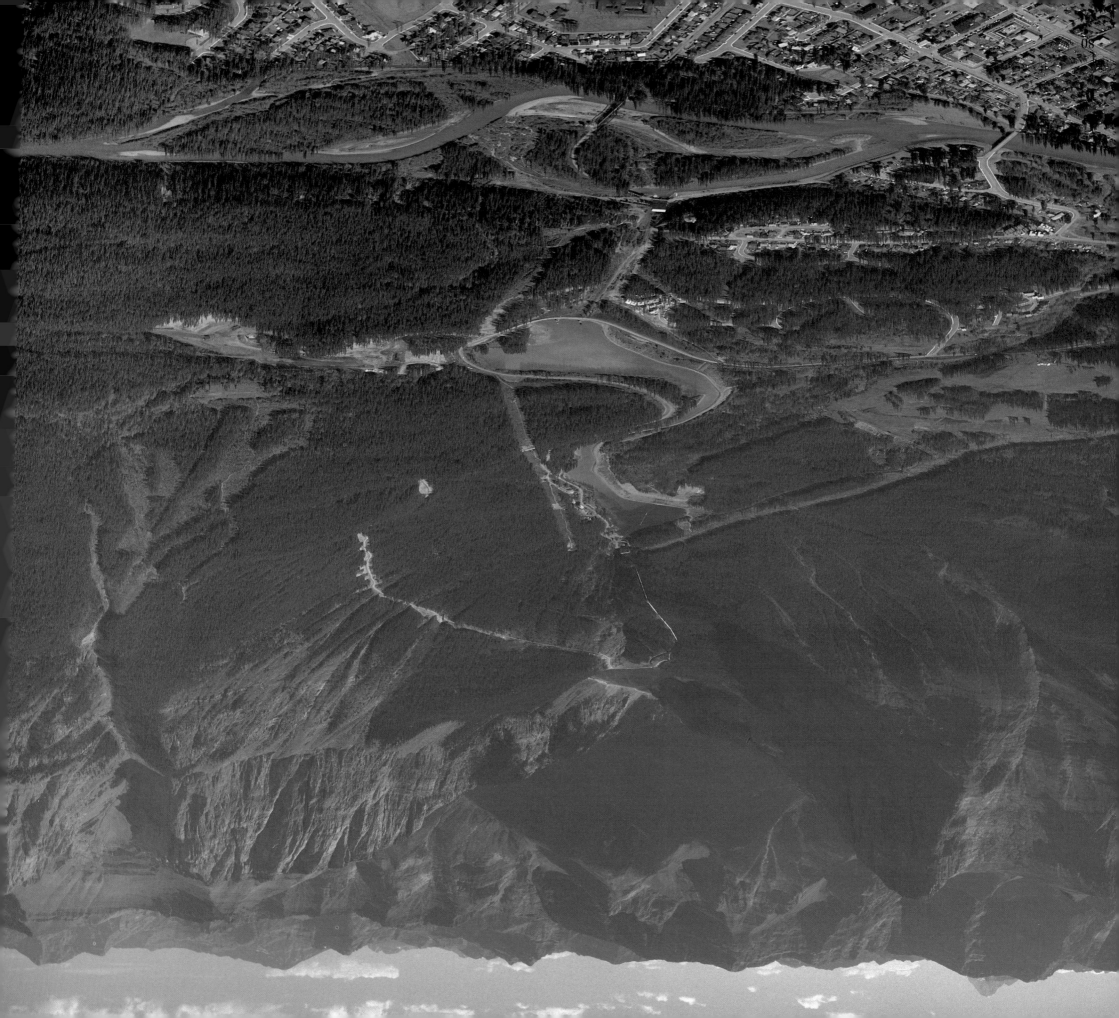

Alberta. Calgary (these pages and overleaf) was founded as a fort of the North West Mounted Police in 1875 and has grown with startling speed in the intervening years. It is now a bustling city of some 700,000 inhabitants, chiefly concerned with the oil business and with serving the surrounding agricultural area.

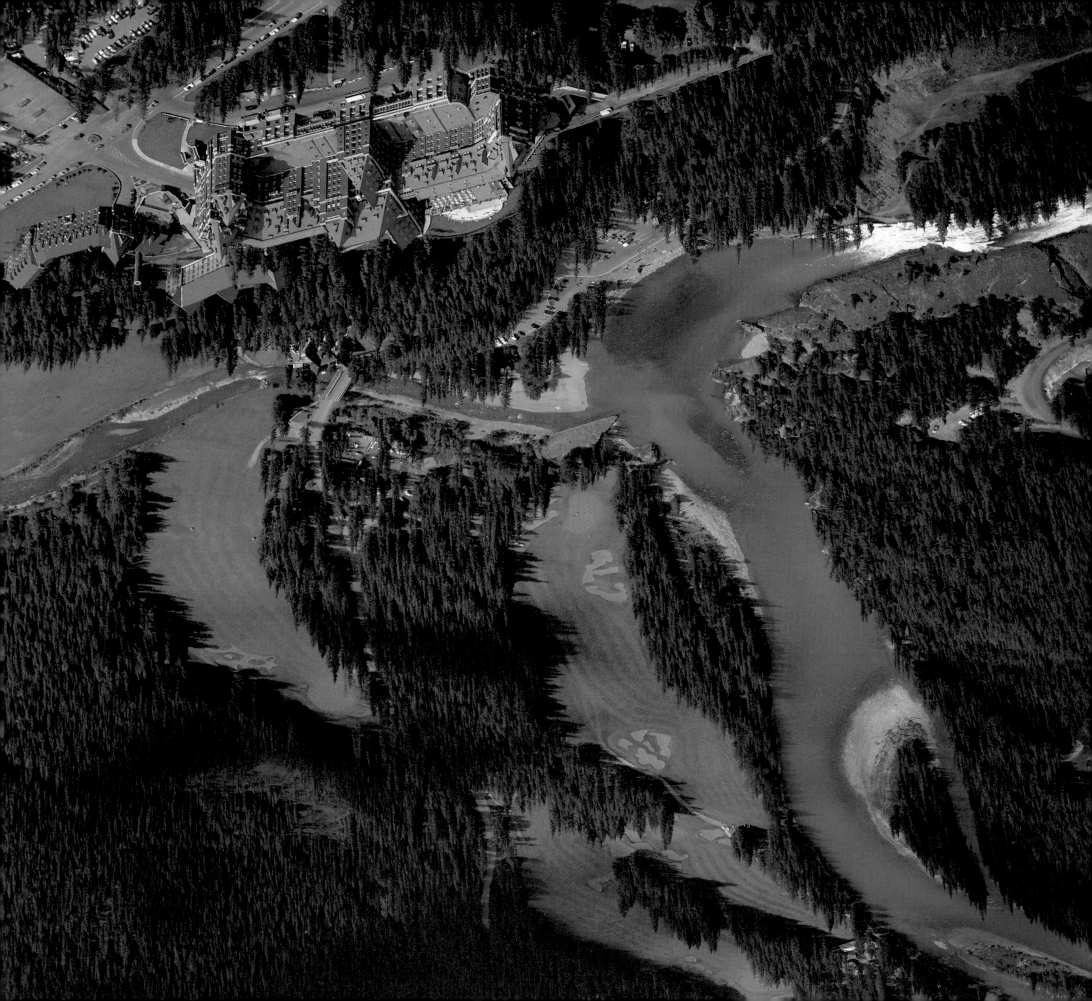

Alberta. These pages: the running waters of the Red Deer River, a tributary of the South Saskatchewan River, which rises near Mount St. Bride, have cut a deep channel through the fertile farmland around Drumheller.

Saskatchewan. Previous pages: (left) sandbanks divide the flow of the Saskatchewan River near Saskatoon, and (right) grain elevators at Broderick. Above: the blue waters of the 50-mile-long Last Mountain Lake, which stretches across the prairies north of Regina. Facing page: the flat lands near Holdfast.

Northwest Territories. With a population of around 10,000, Yellowknife (previous pages right and overleaf) is the largest settlement in the territories as well as their capital. When winter grips the region, the Great Slave Lake freezes to such an extent that a road capable of carrying motor traffic (previous pages left and facing page) is built across the lake to Detah (above), a Dogrib Indian settlement.

Northwest Territories. Mining (above) is the main business of Yellowknife (these pages and overleaf) and was responsible for the two booms in the town's development. The first came in 1934 and resulted in the 'old town' on the narrow neck of land (background, overleaf left), while the second boom, that of the 1950s, created the new town with its more modern buildings (overleaf).

Manitoba was the first of the prairie provinces to be created, coming into existence in 1870 as a small patch of territory around the Red River Settlement. Today, vast areas of the province are under the plough, (these pages) near Dugald and (overleaf left) the Dacotah Farm near Winnipeg, and little is left in its original state. Overleaf right: sunlit waters near Point du Bois.

Manitoba. Above: the graceful loop of an oxbow lake beside the Assiniboine River, west of Winnipeg, is followed by the tracks left by a combine harvester. Facing page: a farm near Winnipeg. Overleaf: the fine, neo-Classical Legislative Building in the heart of Winnipeg. Constructed of local limestone and surmounted by the famous *Golden Boy* statue, the building was completed in 1919 and guided tours are offered to the visitor.

Manitoba. Facing page: the Red River flows through the small town of St. Norbert on its way to Winnipeg (above and overleaf). Winnipeg is the traditional start of the west, lying near the line where the Canadian Shield gives way to the vast, open spaces of the prairies. The city is also vital to the prairies' economy, with its grain exchange, stock yards, railway links and food processing industries.

Ontario. One of the most irregular and beautiful stretches of water in the world must surely be the Lake of the Woods (these pages and overleaf), with its 14,000 islands and long, meandering shoreline. Overleaf right: the town of Kenora, which caters to the needs of the thousands of yachtsmen and fishermen who visit the Lake of the Woods each summer.

Ontario. Thunder Bay (these pages and overleaf) is a major port on the shores of Lake Superior, which handles ships coming through the St. Lawrence Seaway from the Atlantic. The large grain elevators (above) handle some of the vast output from the prairies, while the Great Lakes Paper Mill (facing page and overleaf left) processes great amounts of timber from the interior.

Ontario. The industrial city of Sault Ste. Marie (facing page) stands beside the rapid-strewn St. Mary's River, which connects Lakes Superior and Huron. As part of the St. Lawrence Seaway project, the rapids have been bypassed by a number of huge locks (above and overleaf right) through which pass more than 80 ships a day, carrying 90,000,000 tons of cargo a year, making them some of the busiest in North America. Overleaf left: a smaller lock on a quieter Ontario river.

Manitoba was the first of the prairie provinces to be created, coming into existence in 1870 as a small patch of territory around the Red River Settlement. Today, vast areas of the province are under the plough, (these pages) near Dugald and (overleaf left) the Dacotah Farm near Winnipeg, and little is left in its original state. Overleaf right: sunlit waters near Point du Bois.

Manitoba. Above: the graceful loop of an oxbow lake beside the Assiniboine River, west of Winnipeg, is followed by the tracks left by a combine harvester. Facing page: a farm near Winnipeg. Overleaf: the fine, neo-Classical Legislative Building in the heart of Winnipeg. Constructed of local limestone and surmounted by the famous *Golden Boy* statue, the building was completed in 1919 and guided tours are offered to the visitor.

Manitoba. Facing page: the Red River flows through the small town of St. Norbert on its way to Winnipeg (above and overleaf). Winnipeg is the traditional start of the west, lying near the line where the Canadian Shield gives way to the vast, open spaces of the prairies. The city is also vital to the prairies' economy, with its grain exchange, stock yards, railway links and food processing industries.

135

Ontario. One of the most irregular and beautiful stretches of water in the world must surely be the Lake of the Woods (these pages and overleaf), with its 14,000 islands and long, meandering shoreline. Overleaf right: the town of Kenora, which caters to the needs of the thousands of yachtsmen and fishermen who visit the Lake of the Woods each summer.

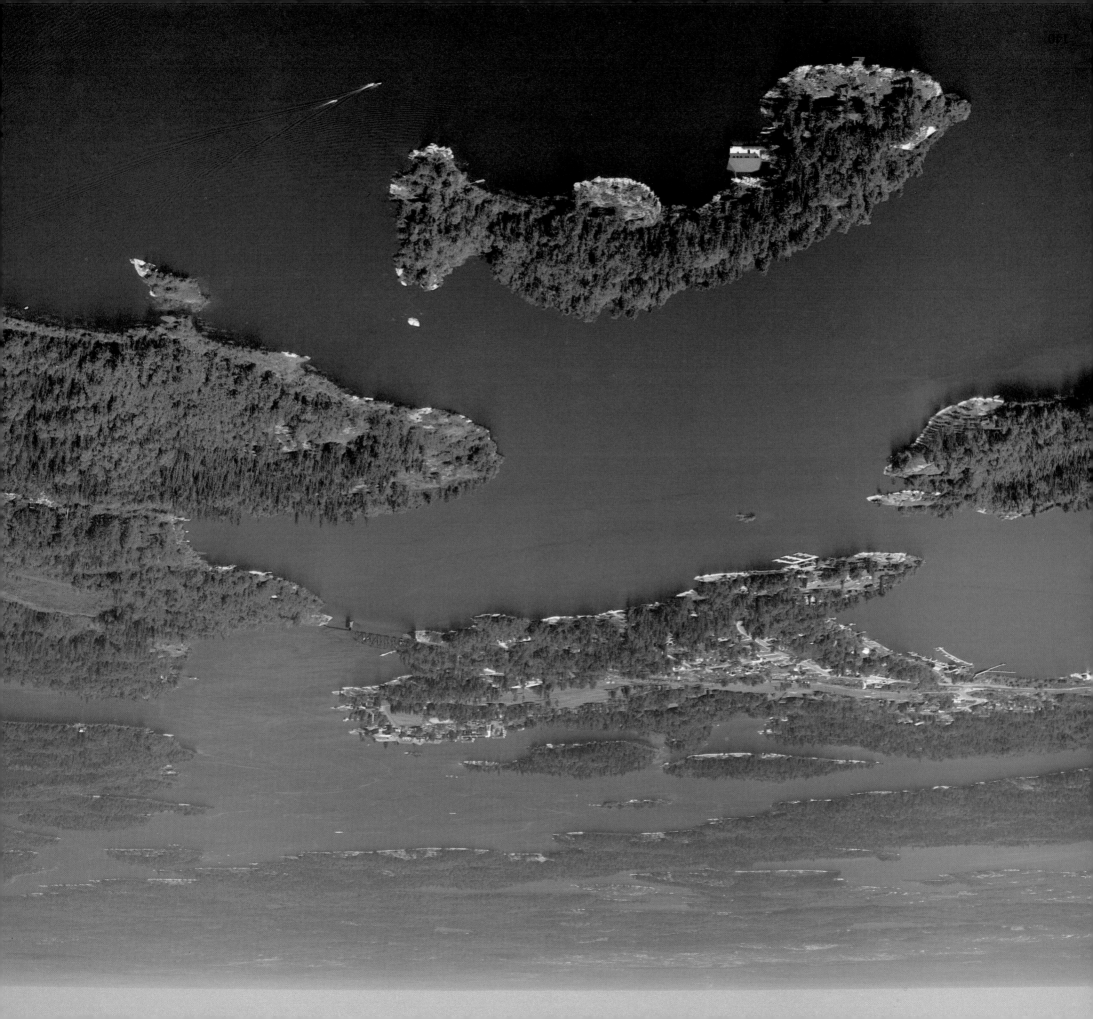

Ontario. Thunder Bay (these pages and overleaf) is a major port on the shores of Lake Superior, which handles ships coming through the St. Lawrence Seaway from the Atlantic. The large grain elevators (above) handle some of the vast output from the prairies, while the Great Lakes Paper Mill (facing page and overleaf left) processes great amounts of timber from the interior.

Ontario. The industrial city of Sault Ste. Marie (facing page) stands beside the rapid-strewn St. Mary's River, which connects Lakes Superior and Huron. As part of the St. Lawrence Seaway project, the rapids have been bypassed by a number of huge locks (above and overleaf right) through which pass more than 80 ships a day, carrying 90,000,000 tons of cargo a year, making them some of the busiest in North America. Overleaf left: a smaller lock on a quieter Ontario river.

Ontario. Above: the blue waters and forested isles of Georgian Bay Islands National Park. Facing page and overleaf left: the *Lady Muskoka* steaming through the scenic waters of Lake Muskoka, north of Gravenhurst. Overleaf right: a country road runs purposefully across fertile fields near Singhampton.

Ontario. These pages: the *Maid of the Mist* boats nose into the turbulent waters beneath the crashing cascades of Niagara Falls, which tumble 160 feet from the escarpment. Overleaf: (left) the intersection of the Macdonald-Cartier Freeway and the Don Valley Parkway, north of Toronto city centre, and (right) Canada's Wonderland, Toronto.

Ontario. Toronto (these pages and overleaf) is a busy, thriving city whose modern skyline, including the distinctive CN Tower (facing page and overleaf), epitomises its prosperity and go-ahead attitude. Above: the Parliament Building in Queen's Park. Facing page and overleaf left: the domes and islands of Ontario Place. Overleaf right: the snow-bound Exhibition Park, where the mighty 'Ex' is held each summer.

Ontario. The Thousand Islands area (facing page and overleaf) of the St. Lawrence River, between Kingston and Brockville, is perhaps the loveliest section of the St. Lawrence Seaway, attracting numerous pleasure craft as well as merchant vessels. Above: the Lake of the Woods.

Ottawa (these pages) was chosen to be the capital of Canada by Queen Victoria in 1857 and, although some contemporaries criticised the choice, it has become one of the most charming and business-like capitals in the world. Above: the neo-Gothic Parliament Buildings constructed between 1859 and 1927.

Quebec. The undulating landscape of Quebec and its harsh winter climate make it ideal for those interested in winter sports, and several resorts have been established to cater to the enthusiast. Above and overleaf left: Gray Rocks. Facing page: the summit of Mont Tremblant. Overleaf right: a ski lift at Mont-Ste-Anne.

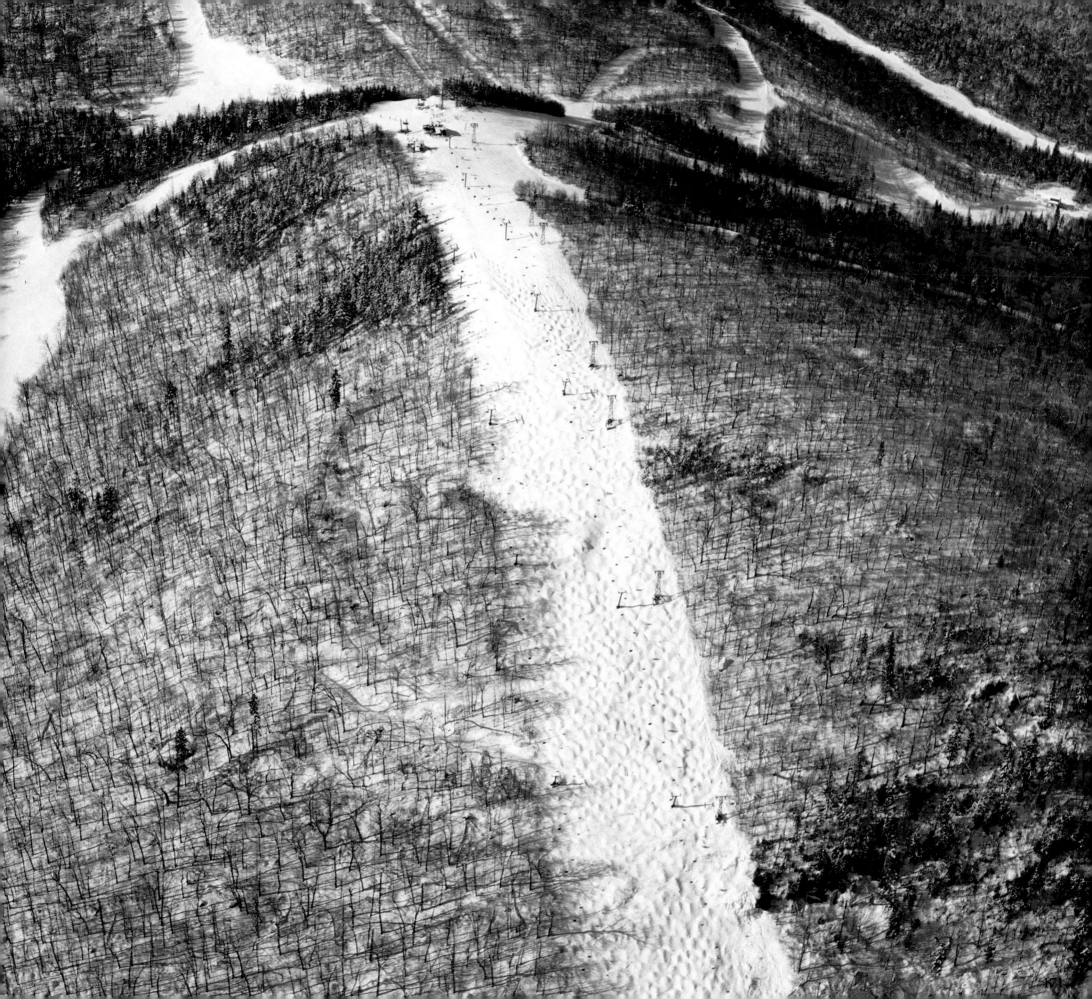

Quebec. The maintenance of the province's ski slopes requires the clearing of trees from long pathways on the hills and some careful work on the part of the staff. Facing page, and overleaf: Mont-Ste-Anne. Above: Stoneham Ski Resort.

Quebec. The oldest part of Quebec City stands on top of, and at the base of, the high bluff which marks the narrowing of the St. Lawrence River and occupies a vital strategic position. The city is almost totally French in its language and culture, maintaining the air of an old French town, with its distinct quarters and narrow, winding streets.

Quebec. Facing page and overleaf right: the rising towers and turrets of the Chateau Frontenac dominate the Upper Town of Quebec City. Built in 1893, this hotel stands on the site of the governor's residence and enjoys some of the finest views in the city. Above: the new area of Quebec, totally geared up to the demands of the 20th century. Overleaf left: the ice palace and snow sculptures which are such a feature of winter's Carnaval.

Quebec. The ice palace and snow sculptures illuminated as a February dusk falls on the city. Facing page and overleaf left: the Chateau Frontenac and Terrasse Dufferin together with part of the Lower Town. Overleaf right: the suspended Pont Pierre Laporte and cantilever Pont de Quebec, just upstream of the city.

185

Québec. Percé (these pages) is a popular resort village, based on an old fishing community surrounded by dramatic cliffs and headlands, the beauty of which attracts thousands of visitors.

Newfoundland. Previous pages: (left) the Humber Valley and (right) Deer Lake. Above: forested scenery south of the Humber Valley. Facing page: a river near North Rustico. Overleaf: (left) the city of St. John's, which began life as a 15th-century fishing port and still handles fishing craft to this day, and (right) Quidi Vidi.

Newfoundland. Above: the rugged headland of Cape Spear, near St. John's. Facing page: Signal Hill, which dominates one side of the narrow entrance to St. John's Harbour. On top of the hill stands the stone Cabot Tower of 1897, which was built to celebrate the 400th anniversary of John Cabot's voyage and is now one of the city's best-known landmarks.

Prince Edward Island. Charlottetown (these pages) is the capital of Prince Edward Island and stands in the heart of a rich agricultural region whose products it exports to the rest of Canada and the world at large. Overleaf: (left) Stanhope Bay and (right) nearby farmland.

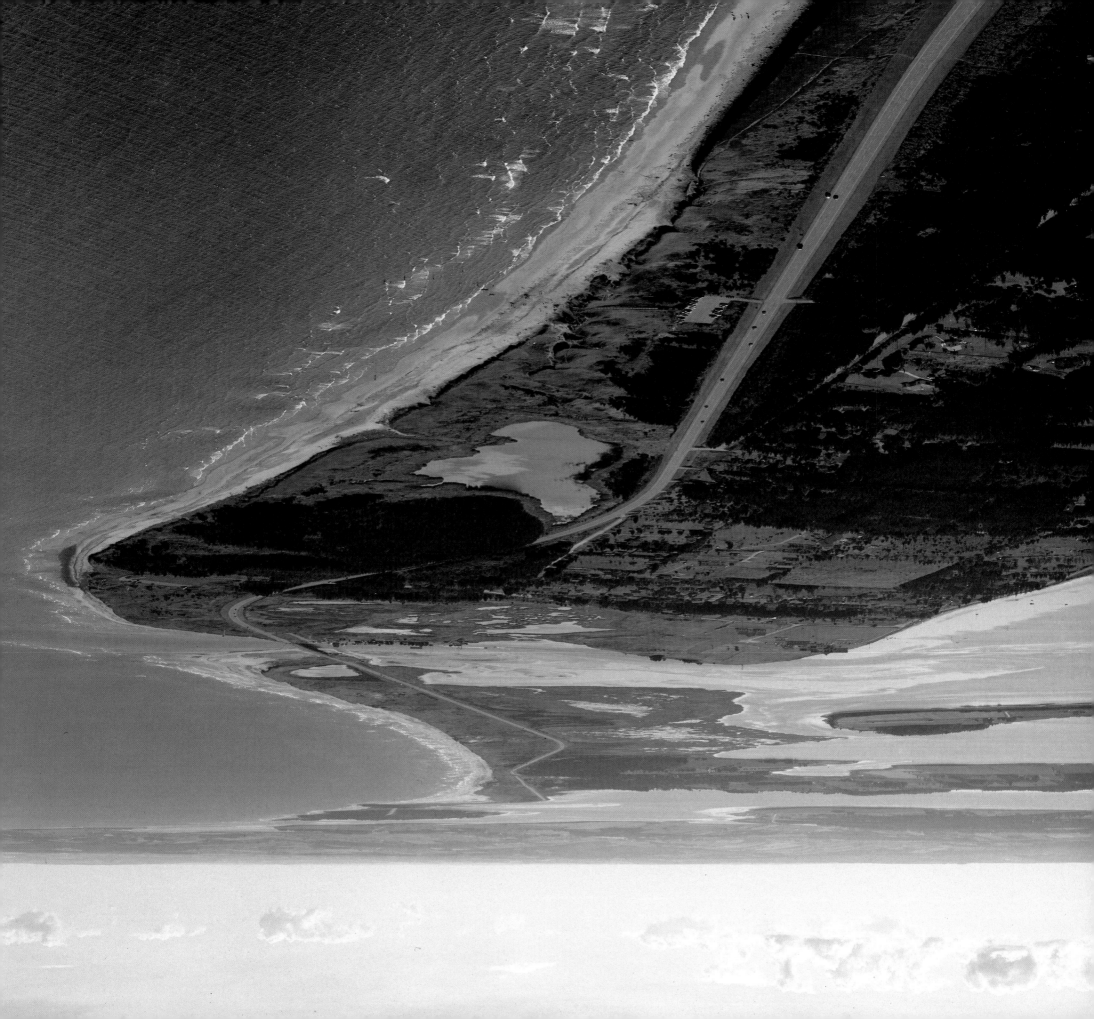

Above: some of the fertile farming land for which Prince Edward Island is so famous. Facing page: part of the Prince Edward Island National Park, near North Rustico Harbour. Overleaf: (left) Port Elgin and (right) the city of Saint John, which has seen a great amount of urban renewal in the past 20 years, both in New Brunswick.

ova Scotia. Previous pages: (left) the Annapolis Valley and (right) Halifax, with the Old Town Clock and fortified
itadel Hill behind the high-rise buildings of the city centre. Facing page: Lunenburg, which has long been one of the
ost important fishing ports in Canada and hosts the annual Lunenburg Fisheries Exhibition. Above: the tiny settlement
f Prospect. Overleaf: Point du Bois, Manitoba.